Secrets Within

PRIMAL VERSES

ZERO ~~TO~~ ONE
2

VOLUME · I

.1+1-1

ANDREY

ALESHINTSEV

AJION PRESS · NEW YORK · 2025

PRIMAL VERSES: VOLUME 1
Zero to One

A PRESS
JION

Published by Ajion Press

An imprint of Ajion Corporation
www.ajion.org

Library of Congress Catalogin-in-Publication Data

Names: Aleshintsev, Andrey, author.
Title: Primal Verses : zeto to one / Andrey Aleshintsev.
Series: Primal Verses Series, Volume 1.
Description: New York : Ajion Press, 2025.
Identifiers: ISBN 979-8-9996794-0-6 (paperback) | ISBN 979-8-9996794-1-3 (hardcover)
ISBN 979-8-9996794-2-0 (ebook) | ISBN 979-8-9996794-3-7 (audiobook) |
ISBN 979-8-9996794-4-4 (b&w paperback) | ISBN 979-8-9996794-5-1 (b&w hardcover)

Subjects: LCSH: American poetry–21st century. | Religious poetry, American. |
Spiritual life–Poetry. | Meditation–Poetry. | Self-actualization
(Psychology)–Poetry. | Personal transformation–Poetry.

Classification: LCC PS3601.L47 P75 2025 | DDC 811/.6–dc23 | BISAC POE005000
SEL032000 REL062000
LC record available at https://lccn.loc.gov/2025925036

First Edition, 2025
Primal Verses Series, Volume 1

Book designed by Andrey Aleshintsev with special thanks to Ajion for the art, @ajion

Every soul carries ancient wisdom,
your truth awaits within these pages.
Three paths, one sacred journey home.

Andrey Aleshintsev

62 : CHAPTERS

Primal Verses   Passport

  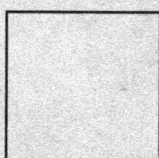

 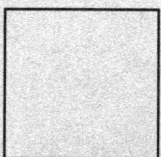 

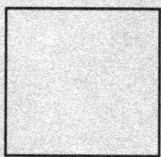  

  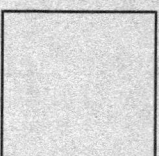

 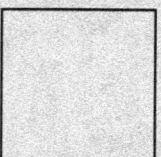 

 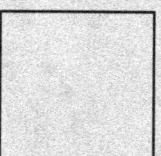 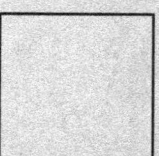

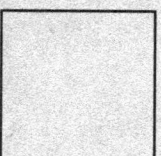 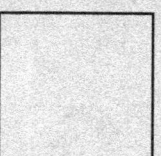 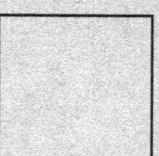

ENHANCE
YOUR READING
EXPERIENCE

Audio and video content is available to complement each chapter. The Primal Verses mobile app provides immersive multimedia content designed to deepen your journey and experience the author's complete vision.

Visit: www.primalverses.com/app

JOIN THE
COMMUNITY

Visit **primalverses.com** to connect with fellow readers, share your own verses, and explore deeper meanings within each chapter.

Primal Verses   Callsign

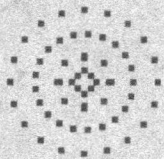 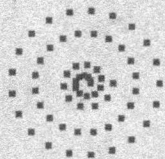 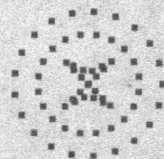

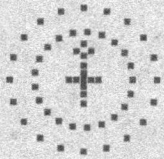  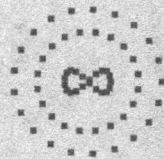

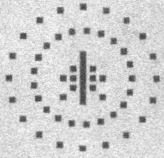 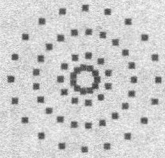 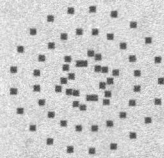

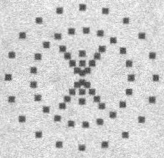 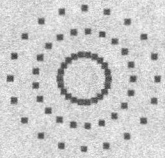 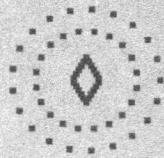

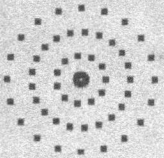  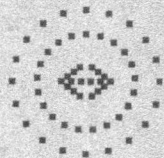

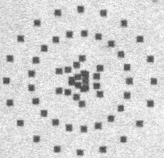 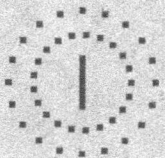 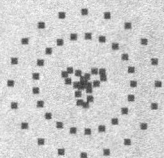

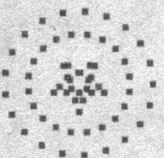 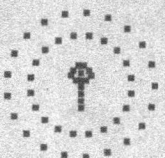 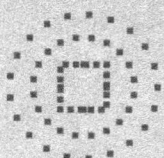

CHAPTER ZERO

"In the void before first breath,
Before the word, before the light,
Dreams the primal architect—
The Zero, longing for the One."
- The Beginning's End

Before the One dwells the perfect void,
Where forms of matter are destroyed,
Yet in this space of pure negation,
Blooms the seed of all creation.

Chapter: Zero

Zero is the center of the wheel,
The axis of all motion,
The blank page where the poet sings,
The space between what IS and what I am.
In nothingness, the something stirs,
Like dreams that wake within the mind,
Where every "is" and "was" occurs,
And time itself becomes untwined—
For Zero holds what One cannot—Infinity.

The One needs its void to hold,
The song needs silence to be heard,
From empty space, all stories are told,
From nothing comes the living word.
Zero is the source within
Where spirit's journey can begin.

What Zero holds, One must embrace:
To know oneself requires Many,
As God needs souls to know Its grace,
So trillions of cells help the Self to find—
Through Many, the One is defined.

The poet knows this ancient art,
From silence, every word is born,
As Zero's sleep makes One awaken,
And the binary world begins to turn.

Before you were, the Zero waited,
After you're gone, it will remain,
In its embrace, ALL IS created,
In its silence: no loss, no gain.

***

Zero is the paradox solved:
To be nothing is to be All,
To be One is to be Many,
And out of Many—God is born.

THE CROSSROADS OF THREE SOULS

You stand at the threshold of transformation, three ancient paths diverge into the depths of human experience. Each path has called to souls throughout time, and one calls to you now. Listen to your inner voice as you read these invitations:

The Seeker whispers: "Come, seeker of truth. Walk with me through the void to the source of all things. We shall descend through consciousness itself, from the highest unity to the deepest spirit. Your soul hungers for transcendence—I will show you the way beyond ordinary reality."

The Wanderer calls: "Join me, explorer of hearts. We'll journey through every emotion, every human experience that shapes us. From purpose to family, through courage and fear, love and loss. Your soul learns through feeling—I will guide you through the beautiful complexity of being human."

The Sage offers: "Walk beside me, seeker of wisdom. Together we'll climb from life's questions to enlightenment's answers. Through truth and illusion, joy and sorrow, choice and destiny. Your soul yearns for understanding—I will illuminate the path to profound wisdom."

Which voice speaks to your soul?

Trust your instinct. Your soul recognizes its path.

THE SEEKER
Quest for Truth & Unity

Turn to **Page 246** for
Chapter 61 : One
Follow Seeker Path

THE WANDERER
Experience & Discovery

Turn to **Page 10** for
Chapter 2 : Purpose
Follow Wanderer Path

THE SAGE
Wisdom & Enlightenment

Turn to **Page 14** for
Chapter 3 : What is life?
Follow Sage Path

Follow your chosen soul symbol.

Primal Verses

Chapter 1
Puzzle of Love

"The dreams of you are scattered.
I wish I never have to dream,
For my soul can be with thee,
Forever."
- Angel's Dream

Why have you charmed my soul?
What purpose do I serve you?
How easily my heart is dominated!
Aching to have my Angel C...

Chapter 1: The Puzzle of Love

The winds of dreams are bending me
To feel my own will,
But the will of mine is trapped
Inside your heart.
How can I think?
Without the vision of your eyes
That pierces my mind to weep
Of how I miss thee.

Passion, dream and hope
Are no longer my thoughts,
But emotions that consume
Me of you!

Your divinity tears me apart,
And flames seduce my mind
To touch and taste your lips,
And hold your precious body.
While whispering three words...

How do I begin to express the magic,
Which is gifted to me through you?
In the stars... in the wind, and in my voice
All shall feel its sadness,
Like tears that disappear in the wind.

Night Terror has concealed my vision,
And I have lost the sound of your voice.
Deaf and blind, I'll drift the world,
Toward the moment of no return,
Where I can only feel your immanence.

***

My breath will fade away,
But memories and love of mine
Can never perish, while you endure.

Your path is your own
CONTINUE

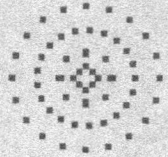

Chapter 2
PURPOSE

"In the end...
All that really matters
Is what you have inspired."
- The Hand of Fate

In the time of war or peace,
We have only one choice to live.
Either master our purpose
Worthy of one's life
Or to submit to life
Of dreamy wishes.

Chapter 2: Purpose

Purpose, purpose on the tree—
Which leaf will it be,
That can change the future?
Draw a million men to fight
Or to have the right to a better life.
A vision that would steal the faith from God,
And be given to humankind.

The idea, the vision, and the future
Will haunt anyone
Who dares to merge these three
In the waking land.

A simple thought that breaks the unworthy
Ideals for all who wish to strive—
An idea that is godly.
And all who live it,
Will know its might.

All prophets had a vision.
A vision that they thought was right.
But the vision that awoke in all mankind,
Is worth more than all the prophets.

Hah, fortune, luck and chance,
Uncertainty that we all fear.
The future is like a cold space—
Vast and dangerous;
But life without adventure—
Is it life?

***

I see it now!
Men in space, colonized and advancing.
Humanity, with a purpose.
An Era of Tau.

Wanderer turn to page 18
Chapter 4 : Dream Seeker

Chapter 3
What is Life?

"Spirits bowed their last energy,
In hope to restore order.
Little did they know
That the heaven's gate has collapsed..."
-Angel's manuscript passage 25

When the days no longer fill us,
With the joy of living.
And every passing moment,
Becomes a bitter taste of air.

Chapter 3: What is life?

One must ask oneself.
What is the purpose of the living?
To live and die?
Or maybe fall in love?
It doesn't matter.
Some seek knowledge,
And others seek the Power.
But what I do know
Must be inside of me forever.

The passion, lust and life
Are all but one, still calling.
To think beyond our simple minds,
That drove us all to fire.

We cannot stop our breathing,
And even if you could?
Would you choose your death
In such a manner?

I say "we breathe a little longer,
And taste the air.
So that one day, in final moment.
We will let go of our precious body,
And see how wonderful we are".

Few will regret a lot of things.
Some will think and simply smile.
Others will forever dream
Of what they were and
What they have become.

***

I'll never leave nor disappear.
Because one day...
We'll read and understand
That our lives are free of fear...

Sage turn to page 42
Chapter 10 : Sacred Wounds

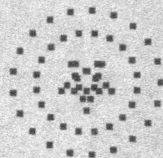

Chapter 4

Dream Seeker

"Cough of blood and burst of pain,
Rips through skin of dying angel...
Hummed last prayer and cursed his...
Maker..."
- Angel's manuscript, passage 43

Bloody trees weep their silent horror,
As an empty sky watches over us.
No god will dare to look inside
Where lost souls are forsaken.

Chapter 4: Dream Seeker

He always feared waking up.
Not knowing if it's still his life.
He sketched it in his head; no smile.
This blurred world drained his final sanity.
Another night—same fear.
He hasn't slept in years.
The eyelid's hinge becomes his gate;
Each dawn arrives as borrowed time.
He swallows a dozen blue pills; he fades.

Fear and horror—monstrosities all—
The soil remembers every scream;
They are near; he can hear their howl.
The earth is bloody, torn with flesh.
From creatures only pure evil sees.

Deep breath, the beat of his terrified heart;
An ill mind and bleeding eyes.
A feeling carried all his life—
Irresistible, a drug of fire,
Pure madness driving men to death—or worse, insanity.

Mountains of dead bodies,
Every kind of creature bleeding
Warm blood running to the core—
Either this world drinks or dies,
This realm feeds on innocent blood,
Of its undying residents.

He is stranded in this desecrated land,
Alone—armed with bare fists.
Fighting the same nightmare he always feared,
But this time he knows it's real.

***

"Doctor, will he ever wake up?"
"I am afraid it is up to him."
Four years later, the heart went silent.

Wanderer turn to page 22
Chapter 5 : Anger

Primal Verses

Chapter 5
Anger

"Flames of wrath consume the soul,
Like a tempest in darkened skies.
Each breath ignites another fury,
Till nothing remains but ashes..."
- Whispers of the Damned

When thunder strikes the mortal heart,
And reason drowns in crimson tide,
We become the monsters we feared,
In mirrors of our own design.

Chapter 5: Anger

One must taste the bitter flame,
That burns beneath our mortal skin.
It consumes like a hungry demon,
Devouring peace with a savage grin.
As wrath's weight bears down,
And fury's poison seeps in deep,
Oh, how it transforms our essence,
Into tempers we cannot disguise,
With anger as our guide.

The blood runs bright with rage,
While thoughts grow sharp and brutal,
Each moment breeds fresh agony,
As fury floods our hearts:
This feast of bitter pain
That locks the heart in iron cage.

Savage beast within us all,
Awaits its moment to emerge.
When sanity abandons the mind,
Fury claims its rightful throne—
We become what we despise.

Rage whispers ancient tales
Of power that corrupts the soul;
It promises sweet revenge,
But leaves us hollow—ash.

Through blazing fury we carve our path,
To tame the furnace from within.
For anger burns without wisdom,
Until we bend it to our will.

***

In wrath's domain or love's sweet rest,
We choose the path our hearts will take.
But fury left to grow unchecked
Leaves only ashes in its wake.

Wanderer turn to page 26
Chapter 6 : Memory

CHAPTER 6
MEMORY

"Forgotten voices softly sing,
With stories bathed in silver light.
Each memory holds what once was dear,
To those who are no longer here."
- Keeper of Lost Times

When memories flood the silent mind,
Like autumn leaves on a gentle breeze,
We drift between what was and is,
In realms of timeless reveries.

Chapter 6: Memory

One must wander through the mist,
Through countless moments swept away.
Where joy and sorrow intertwine,
Like lovers in an endless dance.
These phantoms of the past
Still haunt our waking dreams.

Each memory holds sacred truth,
Preserved in the amber of the mind.
Some as sweet as morning's tender kiss,
Others sharp as broken glass.
They shape the essence of our souls,
With whispers soft and cruel.

Time's current sweeps along,
Through valleys carved by grief and joy.
These waters show our past—
The former dreams and ghosts,
Not yet ready to be forgotten.

Precious moments slip away,
Like grains of sand between our fingers.
We grasp at fading images
That blur with each passing day.
Until the truth becomes a myth,
And myths become our truth.

Within the castle of the mind,
We guard the relics of our years.
Some chambers echo with our pain,
While others hold forgotten tears.

***

We journey through this life,
With moments left behind.
These memories connect
The heart, the soul, the mind.

Wanderer turn to page 58
Chapter 14 : Jealousy

CHAPTER 7
SPIRIT

"We walk upon the Terra,
Blind to the spirit within,
Which defines our Ego."
- Men and women of the Earth.

The Abyss looks back into our eyes,
As we search for salvation;
Science and faith go blind,
Lost in the illusion of matter.

Chapter 7: The Spirit

One must feel the presence of the spirit,
For the sleeper must be awakened.
It may take millions of noble souls,
But if they all strive for one conclusion,
Then sacrifice is absolute.
The human spirit of the chosen
Will rise again to show the truth.

The feeling, the emotion and the mind
Are elements of an inner spirit.
We must be taught and guided,
However ignorant people may be.

We feel duality in life
To cry and to laugh.
The world is made this way,
Yet truth abides within the One;
Oneness—a boundless feeling—
Is the energy lying inside us.

Emotion strikes like thunder;
We know when we have lost control.
Yet One must not feel guilty.
This drive is the essence of our life;
Without it, we are not ourselves.

Our mind is more powerful than we imagine,
An instrument of the Gods we barely know;
Our thoughts and our ideas
Are blurred reflections of their dreams.

***

Our spirit does not die,
Nor does it disappear.
It sleeps in neither hell nor heaven,
Until it is ignited once again.

Seeker turn to page 250
CONTINUE

Primal Verses

CHAPTER 8
I EXIST

"Are we aware of ourselves?
While the mind is consumed by the noise
Of the outside world."
- Mystic

In darkness or in light,
Will the human mind let go
Of the idea that the universe
Was not created for us alone.

Chapter 8: I exist

One must ask oneself.
How do I know that I exist?
I know because I feel it,
And others feel it too.
Are we deluded? It cannot be.
I see the stars,
And worlds within them—
O boundless Universe, I know!
I do exist.

The past, the future, and the present
Hold the keys we seek,
To doors of our existence.
Behind their mystic locks
We listen, patient and humble,
And find what waits within.

When time slips through our hands,
Only memory and story remain,
Telling how things were,
So we can mend the road ahead
And build a kinder future.

Until then, let us not destroy
What we are sworn to tend;
Or we may never see the day
When our children play again.

Now, in this very moment,
I gaze into the moon's eclipse,
And in its quiet tidal dark,
My doubts disappear.

***

Although we long to live forever,
I'm glad that we do not.
Mortality makes meaning real,
And simply being is enough.

Seeker turn to page 30
Chapter 7 : Spirit

Chapter 9
Flesh

"This flesh of mine, so brief, so frail,
Will tell its story, then grow pale,
Each beating heart counts down the days,
A mortal dance in finite ways."
- Testament of The Living Body

In flesh we find our earthly home,
Where spirit learns to breathe and roam,
This temple built of blood and skin,
Holds mysteries within.

Chapter 9: Flesh

One must embrace this borrowed clay,
Our earthly lease from day to day.
These hands that work, these feet that roam,
And shape the world we call our own.
The body bears both joy and ache,
Each breath a gift we daily take.
Though time will claim this mortal frame;
We honor flesh without shame,
And bless the earth from which we came.

How strange to dwell in mortal shell,
Where joy and sorrow rise and swell;
These cells pulse with sacred power,
This flesh that heals with each new hour.
Mistreat the body—pay the price,
But honor it, and life feels right.

The body teaches what words cannot,
Through pain and pleasure, cold and hot.
Each scar becomes a lesson learned,
Each tender kiss our hearts have earned,
Through countless cells we breathe and grow.

Cells pulse anew with morning's light,
The body heals through day and night.
This flesh regenerates and mends,
A quiet miracle we own.

This temple built of dust and breath,
Will teach us life, will teach us death.
In flesh we find what hearts can hold,
Before our spirits break the mold.

***

From dust we rise, to dust return,
Yet in between, sweet love we learn.
Our flesh becomes the sacred scroll,
Where God reads stories of the soul.

Seeker turn to page 34
Chapter 8 : I Exist

CHAPTER 10
SACRED WOUNDS

"We bear the marks of love and loss,
Each scar a window to the soul.
Where pain becomes our holy cross,
And age brings wisdom to our youth."
- Chronicles of the Heart's Ascension

In valleys deep where angels weep,
We crawl toward redemption's shore,
Each wound becomes a promise kept,
A path worth living for.

Chapter 10: Sacred Wounds

One must embrace what cuts us down,
The blade that carves our destiny.
Beneath what we must bear,
Our stronger self emerges.
And wounds become the prayer
Where the broken spirit surges—
We find the strength to rise
Beyond our mortal cries.

Between the moments when we break,
We find the pieces of our truth.
Each fragment frames the choice we make,
Where wounds become our sacred proof.
Until our spirit learns to see
The beauty in our fragility.

Our bodies hold each painful story
Of moments that once tore us wide.
From fragments we assemble glory—
An art that fills us with pride,
Like stained glass where angels hide.

Through tears, we wash away the old
And make room for the new.
Each wound becomes a hand to hold
As we discover what is true.

What breaks us down can build us up,
If we embrace the sacred fall.
The heart that's known what can go wrong
Learns to treasure what is small.

***

In sacred wounds, we plant the seeds
Of all we're meant to be.
The pain that brings us to our knees
Can set our spirits free.

Sage turn to page 50
Chapter 12 : Forgiveness

Primal Verses

Chapter 11
Faith

"In darkness, faith shall light our way,
When sight fails at the close of day.
The sacred fire within burns bright
To guide our steps through endless night."
- Whispers of the Eternal Soul

When shadows cloud our weary minds,
And certainty begins to break,
We reach beyond mortality
To touch infinity.

Chapter 11: Faith

One must trust the force within,
Where reason ends and faith begins,
A sacred leap into the unknown,
Where doubt and hope unite as one,
Faith forms the shield of whispered prayer,
Both holy armor and faithful guide,
The leap of trust through empty air,
That leads beyond what mortals see—
The path to immortality.

Faith blooms where sacred questions grow—
Why do we love through joy and woe?
Why hope when hope appears to die?
Why dream of realms beyond the sky?
Why trust in what we cannot prove?
Faith is the force that makes us move.

When life feels meaningless and vain,
Faith sees beyond our mortal pain,
Each soul the Maker holds with care,
The faithful trust without despair,
And march ahead without fear.

Faith arms us for the fight within,
Makes soldiers of the meek and mild,
Transforms our losses into triumphs,
And keeps the spirit undefiled.

Past reason's edge, faith makes its home,
Dancing free where spirits roam,
Trust unveils what the soul must see
In realms of pure infinity.

***

Faith pierces armor made of pride,
Conquers all with sacred might,
Nothing left for doubt to hide—
Death folds into eternal light.

Seeker turn to page 38
Chapter 9 : Flesh

Chapter 12
FORGIVENESS

"Chains of sin bind heart to heart,
Words of grace grant a fresh new start.
Mercy's sword cuts bondage free,
Now we both can simply be."
- Laments of the Dawn

From ash we rise, hearts aflame,
Hands trembling without shame.
In pardon's art we find our way,
To breathe anew this very day.

Chapter 12: Forgiveness

One must touch the sacred hurt,
Speak the truth of inner pain,
Shake the guilt like gathered dirt,
Let its darkness seep right through,
Forgive the sins both great and small,
Help the broken heart aspire,
Sing a song that heals us all,
Where the wounded souls acquire
All the peace that they desire.

The mirror trembles, secrets spill,
From depths where hidden sorrows rest.
Each throb of ache becomes a star
To guide the soul through every test.
Only the pain that finds its voice
Can heal what hurts deep within.

Let anguish pour like cleansing rain,
Wash scarlet marks from the burdened mind.
Release dissolves our bitter stain,
Each sigh ascending, unconfined,
Where forgiveness blooms to life.

We burn like a phoenix from the ash,
Teach hearts to love and trust again.
What withered finds a place to heal,
And hope revives the mind.

Wounds become the path to peace,
Weight dissolves like melting snow.
Mercy heals what hate destroys,
Joy transforms our bitter pain.

***

In letting go we stand as One,
The wounded, weary, lost in pain.
Our kindness shines like morning sun
And teaches hearts to love again.

Sage turn to page 62
Chapter 15 : Truth

Primal Verses

CHAPTER 13

THE MIND

"In the beginning was the thought,
And the thought became awareness,
And awareness became the world,
When awareness found its voice."
- Ancient Wisdom

When consciousness first stirs awake
In neurons of the infant brain,
The mind begins its endless quest
To map the vast unknown terrain.

Chapter 13: The Mind

One must find the center,
Where thoughts and thinker meet,
The mind that knows its knowing
Makes consciousness complete.
Self-awareness is the anchor,
When consciousness takes hold,
The mind can finally break
From patterns grown old,
And watch the Ego—take form.

All seeking ends where it began
In consciousness that knows itself,
While fragments of the greater plan
Transcend the Ego's throne,
The thinking mind becomes the whole
Where awareness meets the soul.

In silence, soul and mind unite,
Revealing who we've always been,
The Ego fades from mortal sight,
As consciousness lets truth come in—
And self awakens—to the Ethereal.

Yet still the mind creates its forms:
Creator, killer, judge, and jury,
Mind unleashes love and fury,
Builds cathedrals, forges chains,
Then laments what it ordains.

From origin to the journey's end,
Mind traces circles ever wide,
Until all paths converge
At the Source that lies within.

***

The mind's grand cycle, rise and fall,
Expanding—then returning to the conscious void,
In life's embrace or death's final call,
We end where we began—still learning.

Seeker turn to page 46
Chapter 11 : Faith

Primal Verses

Chapter 14
Jealousy

"Whispers carry on the breeze,
Jealous secrets, bitter lies.
They shake the strongest loving trees,
Until trust withers and dies."
- Scrolls of the Embered Heart

Venom drips from envy's fangs,
Into hearts that beat with pain.
Sweet affection wanes and hangs,
Like flowers dying in the rain.

Chapter 14: Jealousy

One must know the jealous thorn,
That pierces tender skin.
It leaves our hearts worn,
And lets the darkness in.
But thorns protect the rose,
And pain can teach us well.
So bear what envy shows,
Until we break the spell,
And learn what love can tell.

Jealous gaze, a hungry flame,
Devours a light that isn't ours.
We fear we're not the same,
And count their lucky stars.
But every spark we wish to hold
Burns bright in stories yet untold.

The venom spreads like winter frost,
Chills warm love with icy fear.
It counts each moment joy is lost,
Keeps affection ever far,
Year after year.

Jealous drops fall one by one,
Paint the heart in envious shade.
They say love cannot be won—
So hide it—small, afraid.

Poison drips from jealous eyes,
Stains the ground where trust once stood.
Love, beneath suspicion, lies—
Misunderstood.

***

The jealous heart beats soft and slow,
Then whispers what we need to know:
"I was not love's enemy—
I was love's plea: 'Don't abandon me.'"

Sage turn to page 70
Chapter 17 : Fear

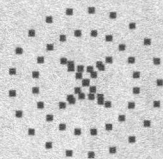

CHAPTER 15
TRUTH

"In God's demise,
We see and understand.
The truth cannot be comprehended.
All things are equal..."
- The forbidden name...unspoken.

The tales of our lives contained,
While darkness clouds our dreams.
We must burst out from the bubble,
And see the truth within.

Chapter 15: Truth

Why do we look no further?
Or have we found our chosen path?
It is delusion—
Yet certainty's false god
Rules with an iron rod.
One must never stop.
The search is never over,
Or we will never know
The hidden secrets of the Cosmos.

Yet the memory, the soul, and a dream—
All dwell within ourselves.
But we are blinded after all.
We won't let go—
One thing without the other.

We pray and beg forgiveness,
But no one hears our call.
The last lord has died,
So long ago.

The memories of men
Were often catastrophic.
The wars and plagues
Are imprinted in their heads.

Oh, how magnificent is our soul.
It is the pure energy of our senses.
Yet often forgotten—
Though it's remembered in the end.

Dreams are our essence.
For we can see
And feel the magic
While we are sleeping.

***

Though few may understand,
That God IS the One.

Sage turn to page 66
Chapter 16 : Lie

CHAPTER 16
LIE

"...Oh, the little lies!
Have you met the Christ?
Did he give you books to read?
And did you read?—oh, the big lies..."
- Dialogue with an Oracle

Since the time of the spoken word,
Humankind became a herd.
Words transformed into language.
Turned thoughts into vantage.
Now words betray their message—
Oh, the menace of the lie.

Chapter 16: Lie

Do you justify or decry the lie?
Too big or too small, it poisons your soul.
Speak up—or shut up—but do not deny
That you love to lie; remember your alibi.
Ask what your fiction costs and why,
What harm it hides, what shame it buys.
We borrow masks to purchase time,
Then wear the mask until it binds—
Now choose the moral for your lie.

Does it kill? Does it make someone cry or laugh?
You couldn't resist; you had to enlist!
We all lie; call it the original sin—
At first a "white" one, paper-thin,
It sweetens speech, then stains the skin,
Until the habit writes itself within.

Why did it kill? Was it God's will? Or was it the banker's bill?
What did you say? Why did you betray? It's cliché anyway!
Too big or too small, it poisons your soul.
Don't deny it—you love to lie.
Remember your Valentine!

Wrong words, wrong name, no one to blame.
You played a con game,
Left with shame and an insurance claim.
Remember tax day?

Am I fat? Am I old? Do you like?
Will you ever stage a sympathy strike?
Stand up; stop being a suck-up—
Speak the truth you fear to write.

***

Save your soul; do not lie.
Let conscience be your why.
Though comfort die, keep language clean—
Original sin will test your reply.

Sage turn to page 126
Chapter 31 : Happiness

Primal Verses

Chapter 17
Fear

"The boy is shattered with fear,
Not able to comprehend the loss
Of his parents."
- Innocent Tragedy

What life is and what life is not,
Without fear in this brief life?
Swift it fades from conscious thought—
Or else corrupts the mind it caught.

Chapter 17: The Fear

One must know what fear is.
The courageous accept it,
And see death ahead.
The craven seek to live forever.
One cannot describe what fear is,
For its uniqueness lies within our own essence.
However, we must learn its purpose.
It steadies hands upon the brink,
And warns the soul before it leaps.

To guard, acknowledge, and decide.
How often we forget these attributes,
That save our lives and define us.
When did we last dare to face
The mirror of our internal scream,
That silent howl within?

An invisible guardian keeps watch.
It cannot be summoned—yet
It appears in times of need.
When all else fails, even hope itself,
Fear will be the bridge to safety or to suffering.

When trembling floods through flesh and thought,
Fear gives us knowledge, cold and keen—
How fragile, how precious this life becomes
When consciousness begs for release.

We understand: we must choose—
A choice both stark and undeniable,
Wield fate, or be wielded toward the grave.
Yet every choice leads toward truth.

***

What is fear, what is it not?
Teacher and destroyer both;
A gift that wounds, a curse that saves—
Embrace the teacher dressed in dread.

Wanderer turn to page 74
Chapter 18 : Courage

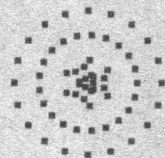

Chapter 18
Courage

"The trembling hand that holds the pen
Can write the words that change the world.
We speak what must be said,
And storm the gates of what must be."
- Records of the Rebellion

When prophets speak of coming night,
And seers warn of endless dark,
We choose to be the morning star,
And step into the great unknown.

Chapter 18: Courage

One must learn the ancient ways,
From warriors long past,
And choose who we are meant to be,
Through every wind-torn test.
The captain of the heart
Must play the hardest part,
And steer through waves that crash and roar,
Where courage makes its pledge
Never to yield to fear.

Courage strikes the anvil hard,
It forges strength from pain,
Drawing out each buried dream
To break fear's binding chain.
Strike true—with hammer's might—
And free your willing mind.

Truth reflects the hero's heart—
Steadfast, strength within.
Cast away each doubt and fear,
Let the spirit rise,
And soar beyond the lies.

Brave hearts forge their dreams;
Step beyond the known.
The abyss yields to those who dare,
Guided by inner light.

Thus courage is no thunderclap—
But steady drumming of the will;
A quiet bond with life,
One broken only by neglect.

***

Heroes leave their footprints
In courage's sacred sand—
Each step a testament
To taking a brave stand.

Wanderer turn to page 78
Chapter 19 : Promise

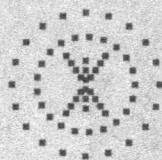

CHAPTER 19
PROMISE

Promises slip like sand,
Easy to lose, hard to collect,
Each grain judges the hand.
- Oathbinder

Dawn reveals what's left to give
Debits of intent against credits of deed;
We tally in quiet breaths,
Hoping silence covers the deficit.

Chapter 19: Promise

One must know a vow's true cost—
Before the words take flight,
See what might be gained or lost,
In darkness or in light,
For promises are bridges built,
On ground of hope or guilt,
Where trust can bloom or wilt,
Before we seal our fate
With promises we dare to keep.

Faithful words stand strong,
Like pillars holding sky;
They right what once went wrong,
Make sacred what we own.
Such promises become our guide,
With honor at our side.

While scattered oaths lie broken,
Like mirrors on the floor;
Each shard a word unspoken,
Trust crumbles under blame;
Speech has nothing left to say.

Self-made promises hold tight,
Whispered soft in empty rooms,
They become our guiding light,
When all other hope is consumed.

The broken word can teach
What whole ones never could;
Sometimes we must breach
To serve a greater good.

***

We end where we began:
With promises in hand,
But wiser now we know
Which ones to let go.

Wanderer turn to page 82
Chapter 20 : Traitor

Primal Verses

Chapter 20
Traitor

"Silver tongues weave velvet snares,
Promises shimmer like poisoned wine.
Beware the smile that blooms too wide."
- Codex of Fractured Vows

When trust sleeps,
The dagger stirs.
Footsteps of betrayal
Echo before the scream.

Chapter 20: Traitor

One must know the traitor's scent,
Long before their fangs catch flesh;
See past jealous tears
That fall like poisoned rain;
Ask if staying mute heals—or harms.
Watch for trembling voices,
Hands that shake when truth draws near;
Hold steady—blink,
You die.

Track the quiver in their voice,
Glances make the coward's choice
To dodge the light of day.
Truth will always find a way,
But betrayal's restless heart
Tears itself apart.

Betrayal's gift is clarity,
With a blade's honesty—
Which bonds hold, which bonds break;
Which souls are false, which souls seek the truth
In all its purity.

The deepest cuts are carved within
The circle we let in.
Guard your inner sanctum well,
But don't become a shell.

Memory plays the scenes again,
Moments when the path was clear.
Could have chosen differently—
Now I'm a prisoner here.

***

The betrayer's heart grows numb,
To the pain of what they've done.
Isolation is the price
For rolling trust's loaded dice.

Wanderer turn to page 86
Chapter 21 : The Murderer

Primal Verses

Chapter 21
The Murderer

"Steel trembles against yielding flesh,
Piercing until silence claims each cry.
Mutilated voices tell their tormented tales—
Of innocent souls who only wished to die."
-Whispers from hell

Hope is losing faith,
Darkness swallows light
From endless suffering within.
The gods have played their cruelest joke.

Chapter 21: The Murderer

Grey days he hated most,
Not that he cared
Whether to breathe, bleed, or vanish.
He'd choose eternal solitude,
But existence held him captive,
And everything he ever wanted
Broke like glass beneath his feet.

Fury and anguish nourish his bones.
He has become the killer,
Dwelling in forgotten places,
Stalking the innocent.

Homeless and heartless,
No companions warm his soul.
Isolation burns around him—
Only blood sustains him now.

Another night, another victim.
He waits like a living shadow.
She wanders, dreaming of tomorrow's promise.
One swift blade-stroke—her heart stops,
Blood cools on steel.

Reality's reflection cracks;
Street corners echo rumors
Of one who murders for joy,
Numb to suffering, blind to dawn.
His own agony compels him
Toward endless, merciless killing.

***

He remained unknown to the world,
But his legacy lay scattered—
Hundreds of bodies in forgotten
Underground tunnels of New York City.

Wanderer turn to page 90
Chapter 22 : Redemption

Chapter 22
Redemption

"Pride must fall before we rise,
Truth cuts deep but cleanses well,
God sees past our worn disguise,
Breaking free from private hell."
- Ledger of the Redeemed

In silence, we learn to hear
The whisper of our worth,
What filled our hearts with fear
Now celebrates rebirth.

Chapter 22: Redemption

One must walk the pilgrim's path
Out of the country of regret
Toward the promised land of peace.
We carry only what we need—
Humility as walking stick,
Compassion as our daily bread,
Hope as water for the journey,
Mercy for the debts we owe;
And love as our blanket.

In the graveyard of old dreams,
We kneel to roll the stones of "never"
And "too late" and "impossible."
By bowing low, we find the strength
To let the light of possibility
Pour through redemption's door.

From the grave of who we were,
New life begins to stir,
Death gives birth to hope,
Teaching broken hearts to cope,
In God's redeeming light.

The wounded learn to heal,
From scars that make them real,
In learning how to forgive
We help others truly live.

From redemption's sacred fire,
We become what we aspire,
Phoenix rising from the ash,
Faith ignites in holy flash.

***

In silence, hear the angels sing
Of second chances mercy brings;
The symphony of souls set free
Echoes through eternity.

Wanderer turn to page 94
Chapter 23 : Awakening

Primal Verses

CHAPTER 23
AWAKENING

"The sleeper's mask falls free,
Revealing what must be.
Behind the mortal face—
Divinity."
- Scrolls of Inner Revelation

The mirror shatters; truth appears,
Washing away a thousand fears,
What once was clouded clears—
Eternity through mortal tears.

Chapter 23: Awakening

One must dive beneath the skin,
Where forgotten gods begin,
Their whispered secrets long concealed;
Crack the armor of the mind,
Leave the sleeping world behind,
Let the hidden self unveil;
Stand naked in the cosmic wind,
Till every pretense thins to none,
And wounds long captive come undone.

Identity melts away,
As body tunes to cosmic hum.
Boundaries blur and fade—
One consciousness displayed.
The Many fold into One,
Beneath awakening's sun.

Consciousness expands like breath,
Inhaling all of space and time.
What seemed like living death
Reveals the paradigm:
All sacred, all sublime.

Eternity bleeds through.
The wanderer finds the God within
In what they always knew—
The One disguised as Two.

Surrender is the key;
It opens what we're meant to be.
The wave returns to sea,
The bound soul breaking free.

***

The dreamer wakes to find
They were the dream itself.
No separate peace of mind—
Only the cosmic Self.

Wanderer turn to page 98
Chapter 24 : The Ordinary Miracle

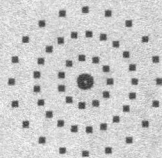

Chapter 24
The Ordinary Miracle

"Coffee steam and morning's kiss,
Her hair a halo, wild and sweet.
In moments ordinary as this,
Heaven and earth quietly meet."
- Mother's Day

When greatness sleeps in simple things,
And beauty dwells in daily bread,
We find ourselves awakening
To miracles we almost missed.

Chapter 24: The Ordinary Miracle

One must pause amid the rush,
Of endless tasks and mounting bills.
In kitchen light at break of dawn,
When children's laughter fills the air.
How quickly moments slip away,
Like water through our grasping hands.
But wonder hides in mundane hours—
In morning coffee, evening walks—
Where joy wears ordinary clothes.

In the cities where we live,
We chase the dreams we think we need;
Each moment guards a treasury,
Of simple joys we fail to see,
Until we stop to recognize
The subtle gold of everyday.

Where children's laughter rings so clear,
The universe reveals its heart;
In what we hold as small and plain
We find our truest, deepest art—
The miracle of being alive.

We race toward distant dreams
While magic waits nearby;
Each moment softly gleams
With wonder we walk right by.

Where dishes wait and laundry piles,
The kitchen light restores our sight;
While a universe of pure joy
Hides in a child's crooked smile.

***

Miracles warm the chipped-clay cup,
In laughter shared and tears wiped dry.
The holy lives in daily toil—
Where raindrops kiss goodbye.

Wanderer turn to page 102
Chapter 25 : Waiting

Primal Verses

Chapter 25
Waiting

"In sterile halls of hope and fear,
Clocks drag their knuckles down the walls.
Each ticking second holds a prayer,
While loved ones wait for news to fall.
- Notes from Hospital Night Shift

When minutes stretch like endless years,
And fluorescent lights buzz overhead,
We live between blind dread and faith,
Suspended by a whispered 'please'.

Chapter 25: Waiting

One must solve the riddle deep,
Of moments that refuse to flow.
Each clue makes weary spirits weep,
While answers hide in depths below.
The puzzle has no final piece,
As torment never finds release.
One searches through the maze of when,
Where questions rise again—and again—
And waiting drives the soul insane.

Seconds stretch like rubber bands,
Each moment snaps and cuts our soul,
We're drowning in time's quicksand,
While waiting swallows us whole.
Fate slips through our trembling hands,
As reason loosens, strand by strand.

Minutes melt like wax in hell,
Each drop scorches our fragile nerves,
Caught inside the waiting spell,
EXIT mocks—worlds apart;
Our sanity dissolves.

Hours drag like broken glass
Across the wasteland of hope,
We're sinking in our darkest fears,
As time dissolves in bitter tears.

The silence screams—
Then—footsteps, curtain, doctor's smile,
The room exhales in collective light.
Time, once torture, whispers "all's well,"
And hearts explode in pure joy.

***

The agony of endless when
Drives mortals to their bitter end.
But waiting holds the sacred key
To what we're truly meant to be.

Wanderer turn to page 106
Chapter 26 : Farewell

Primal Verses

Chapter 26
The Farewell

"Through terminal gates of letting go,
We carry memories like worn bags.
Each goodbye holds a lifetime's weight,
In moments swift as autumn leaves..."
- Letters from Gate B17

When airport lights gleam cold at dawn,
And sleepy travelers drift past,
We find ourselves suspended in
The space between hello and gone.

Chapter 26: The Farewell

One must accept the gift of pain,
When departure calls our name.
In mirrored terminal halls,
We meet who we are, alone.
Through glass that separates two worlds,
Our hearts must train to beat apart.
For distance teaches us to grow,
In solitude we find our strength,
Where farewells forge our truest Self.

We dare to hold the weight of loss,
When departure writes its name in stone.
Past corridors where spirits cross,
We find the strength to stand alone.
In glass reflections, truth appears—
Love deepens through the veil of tears.

When souls depart on wings unseen,
We guard the space where they have been.
Through portraits hung in memory's hall,
Their presence answers when we call,
In silence that no longer hurts.

When weather grounds our planned escape,
And storms remake our careful plans,
We realize that some delays are gifts
That guide where wandering spirits drift.

When departure's bell strikes true,
And calls us to our higher ground,
We remember what we already knew:
That courage can astound.

***

In letting go, we rise to fly
Above the gravity of pain.
For souls who've mastered the goodbye
Find love in loss, and sun in rain.

Wanderer turn to page 110
Chapter 27 : Luck

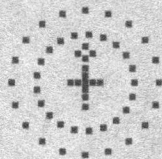

CHAPTER 27
LUCK

"A feather lands on a soldier's boot,
As bullets carve the air around.
He calls it luck—God disguised,
In weightless, perfect timing."
– Field Notes from the Unseen

When luck rewrites the ending,
As fate forgets the plot,
We find ourselves made wealthy
By providence unseen.

Chapter 27: Luck

One must not pray to luck for justice,
Nor treat misfortune as a sin.
It comes uncalled, leaves unexplained,
A silent wind that turns the tide.
A fool may rise with empty hands,
A king may fall with sword in grip—
Both chosen by the same strange drift.

A wrong turn opens sacred doors,
A delayed train births love.
Even the storm we cursed at sea
May carry us to grace.
So much of life is not design,
But driftwood kissed by fire.

Luck is not the prize of good men,
Nor punishment of the bad;
It visits without reason,
And vanishes the same—
So dance with what you're given.

To live is not to make the rules—
But know they're written in the stars.
Still we play like hopeful fools,
And cry through all our scars.

Still we rise and fall like waves,
On nothing more than faith's thin thread,
Yet chance, that neither kills nor saves,
Is fortune's path where gamblers tread.

***

So do not worship luck—
Nor curse its silent exits.
It owes you nothing,
Yet paints your destiny.

Wanderer turn to page 114
Chapter 28 : Broken Heart

CHAPTER 28
BROKEN HEART

A heart does not shatter alone—
It takes the stars and sky with it.
Each crack sings of what once burned,
Now cold and cruel in silent ash.
— From the Forsaken Record

When joy is something we recall,
Not something waiting in the day,
We rise to find the world unchanged—
Except for who no longer stays.

Chapter 28: Broken Heart

One must remember not to call,
When habit reaches for the phone.
Their number waits, like some old spell,
But rings to no one in return.
The voice inside still says their name,
Though months have passed, the ache remains.
We keep their jacket near the door,
Pretend they've only gone to walk—
A lie we use to keep from breaking.

The mirror shows a face unchanged,
Yet something vanished from the eyes.
Laughter echoes far too loud,
As if to drown the missing sound.
We speak to empty rooms that wait,
And smile as if the life still fits.

The world goes on in selfish ways—
With blooming trees and cheerful crowds.
But grief has seasons of its own,
Not tied to clocks or skies or spring.
It settles like a half-said thought,
Too soft to leave, too sharp to stay.

The mug they loved, the book they marked—
All frozen in their final act.
We hesitate to shift a thing,
In fear their presence might fade away.

Still glowing in the grief we hold
Is light no darkness dares to dim.
And though we walk it slow, alone,
We walk it with our love intact.

***

From ashes of what used to be,
What felt like ending, through and through,
A boundless love begins to grow—
Free to embrace what we don't know.

Wanderer turn to page 118
Chapter 29 : Regret

Primal Verses

CHAPTER 29
The Regret

"Regret does not wound, it brands the soul,
With choices burned and never claimed.
Each whispered "what if" haunts the mind,
A shadow engraving our shame."
- Manual for the Cautious Life

When silence builds where love once spoke,
And choices age into remorse,
We find ourselves inside a room
We furnished with the things unsaid.

Chapter 29: The Regret

One must recall the day we judged
Instead of listening, loving, or pausing.
We branded others with our fear,
Too eager to defend our pride.
But once a heart is labeled wrong,
Its trust is not so quick to mend.
We wish we'd asked just one more time—
What hurt, what healed, what mattered then.
But now we grieve—and whisper "sorry."

We chose the path of least resistance,
Convinced that struggle served no good.
But comfort doesn't cure the soul—
It just delays the inner fall.
And what we called "a life well-built"
Now echoes: what might have been.

Truth cut deep, so lies we spoke—
Hoping they'd heal what hurt we caused.
But lies are thorns, not a gentle rose,
And trust, once lost, keeps reaching back
For what we never can undo.

Apologies that took too long
Felt like excuses, not regret.
We offered words, withheld resolve,
And found forgiveness had moved on.

Regret does not erase the past,
It doesn't seek to make us pay—
It brings the past into the now,
And whispers softly: "if only..."

***

Regret will carve you either way—
Into something deeper, or something gone.
Let it break you open—
Not apart.

Wanderer turn to page 122
Chapter 30 : Family

CHAPTER 30
FAMILY

"Cracked roots can cradle bloom,
From violence a lullaby is born.
Family is not who we name—
But who remains when all else fades."
— Testament of Blood and Bond

When the house feels colder with our name,
And the past is folded in a drawer,
Still, a shadow moves in welcome—
Without asking for return.

Chapter 30: Family

One must know that family is messy,
Yet made true.
Not by perfection,
But by presence.
In losses faced together,
And arguments survived.
In birthdays half-remembered,
And hands held through the night.
That's where it lives.

The brother who never said sorry,
But fixed your door.
The mother who held too tight—
And still does.
The uncle who only speaks in warnings,
But never misses your birthday.

Some bonds survive without words,
Some deepen through absence.
Forgiveness may take decades—
Or never arrive.
Yet someone leaves the light on.

Grief, too, belongs to family—
It hides in faded photographs,
In the chair none will sit in,
Proof that love once lived here.

Not all who leave are lost,
Not all who stay are whole.
Yet we grow around the breaks
And bloom in the cracks that raised us.

***

Some return by voice,
Some by memory.
But the door, if ever open,
Means we are a family.

Wanderer turn to page 250
CONTINUE

Chapter 31
The Happiness

"When sunlight breaks through a clouded mind,
And spirit lifts on wings of joy.
We dance in pure, divine delight—
The Self that none can ever destroy."
- Songs of Living Light

To know the world and not oneself,
Is to chase light with closed eyes.
Yet when the gaze turns inward true,
The sun begins to rise inside.

Chapter 31: The Happiness

One must not seek in a stranger's smile,
What lies within the heart's own well.
For joy, when built on outer praise,
Will crumble like a sand-spun shell.
But born within and owned with grace,
It blooms where no permission dwells.
No mirror need reflect your face,
No echo prove the truth you've brought—
You shine enough to light the dark.

In stillness where no crowd applauds,
The soul unfolds its quiet flame.
Neither forged in noise nor fleeting fame,
But rooted deep in love's embrace,
A sacred space where flaws belong,
And wounds find healing in this Light.

Self-worth is not a debt to pay,
Nor prize reserved for perfect days.
It grows when you speak kind and fair—
A quiet rebellion born of grace,
That no one else can give—or take.

Some joy is loud, yet deeper still
Is peace that hums beneath the skin;
It will not flee with loss or pain—
It steadies when the world turns cold.

No crown of gold can match the weight
Of peace that grows ever wiser.
When you become your dearest friend,
Life reveals your very best.

***

So learn to sit with who you are,
And feel your worth in silence swell—
For when you love the Self you keep,
You find the joy you need not seek.

Sage turn to page 130
Chapter 32 : Sadness

Chapter 32
Sadness

"Through corridors of darkened thoughts,
Where tears become the morning dew,
Each sigh escapes like wounded birds
That know the way back home."
— Whispers of Melancholy Heart

When shadows claim the spirit's light,
And joy dissolves in sorrow's reign,
We find ourselves adrift between
The depths of grief and pain.

Chapter 32: Sadness

One must not run from sadness,
It is proof we did not turn to stone.
In trembling hands, it holds the past—
Still warm from when we lived it full.
It dances slow across our bones,
Like music no one else can hear.
Its hush becomes a sacred space,
Where once we broke and still survived,
And nothing false can enter in.

Beneath our calm, the ache resides—
Not broken—just left open wide,
And never quite the same again.
Some truths are heavier than lies,
And settle deep within our bones—
The weight of all we've loved and lost.

The soul remembers what the mind denies:
Moments left unspoken,
Hands never held,
And futures that dissolved in waiting.
Regret is not a thief, but a witness—

Standing silent in memory's court,
Testifying to what was real.
Sadness is not a flaw in joy,
But the echo it leaves behind.
Those who feel deeply—live truly.

Each tear we hold is evidence:
That love once touched us,
That we are not numb,
That feeling is the soul's last vow.

***

We find the courage to remain—
Not to escape, but to feel,
Not to heal, but to honor
What makes us Human.

Sage turn to page 134
Chapter 33 : Illness

CHAPTER 33
ILLNESS

"When breath becomes a burdened tide,
And limbs forget their strength and grace,
The body speaks in quiet codes—
A language born of aching truth."
— From The Book of Living Flesh

When fever melts the mask we wear,
And coughs betray our borrowed strength,
We come to know how frail we are,
And paradoxically, how alive.

Chapter 33: Illness

One must not shun the body's cry,
For illness speaks in sacred tongue.
Each symptom holds a hidden lamp,
Illuminating what we dismissed.
We chase the world, neglecting Self,
Until our health begins to fade.
Then, lying still, we finally hear
The whisper of our weary bones—
"Search for the Self—within."

The ache is not a curse but a guide,
A teacher clothed in trembling skin.
The sweat, the chill, the sleepless dark—
They lead us inward to confront
The parts we've hidden from the Self.
The truth dawns and the Ego falls.

The veil lifts when we lay bare,
Stripped of strength, of pride, of pace.
The pulse of pain becomes a hymn—
It humbles kings and fools alike,
To cradle Self with gentler hands.

There is a grace in being weak.
A gift in being forced to pause.
Where healing is not just repair—
But a full return to the sacred Self.

The body falls to raise the soul.
And what we dread may be the door
Through which our truest life begins.
Illness is not death, but exploration.

***

For even in our weakest hour,
We touch the pulse of something more.
Not death but depth; not end but sign—
That life still fights to be made whole.

Sage turn to page 138
Chapter 34 : Emotion

CHAPTER 34
THE EMOTION

"Before the mind could shape its thought,
The heart had whispered into flame—
A language carved from ache and joy,
Unspoken but complete..."
– Birth of Emotion

When logic paused to feel emotion,
And silence broke beneath the thought,
We entered realms where truth can't lie—
But every impulse is a vow.

Chapter 34: The Emotion

One must surrender to the flood
That rises without name or rule.
Let trembling claim the sacred space
Where thought once seized its clamoring throne.
The soul was never built to be caged,
But born to burn in honest light.
Undo the grip, let silence sing,
And in that roaring depth be found—
Alive, not perfect, but your own.

When pain escapes without a sound,
And breath becomes the only phrase,
One tear will hold a thousand truths—
Unshaped by thought, yet wholly real,
Written in salt upon the skin.

What knowing comes in trembling waves,
When thought has loosened all its hold?
Like amber leaves in restless wind,
Our hearts return to primal verse—
And tears baptize the way to peace.

Amid the cracks of ticking time,
Where raw emotion shapes the world,
We taste eternity made flesh
Within these shells of earth and soul.

For all the wisdom thought may claim,
It's feeling that returns us to our core.
To weep, to burn, to love, to rage—
Is who we are.

***

In feeling's dance, the soul awakes
To weave the thread that never breaks.
For every heart that dares to feel
It stretches time—into the stars.

Sage turn to page 182
Chapter 45 : Coffee

Chapter 35
DEATH

"Last breath escapes like whispered dream
Into the waiting dark
While essence slips through mortal veils
Beyond lament or whispered prayer,
Where silence wraps the conscious void."
– Songs of Final Passage

When flesh gives up
And spirit breaks its chains
We drift between two worlds
Where endings birth beginnings.

Chapter 35: Death

One must arrive where all began,
Where breath once lingered, undefined.
The body fades, but not the thread
That binds us to the conscious whole.
No sorrow follows past the gate—
Only a hush, profoundly known,
Like lullabies we never learned,
But always knew in deeper self.
The soul remembers how to fall.

The final breath, a sacred key,
Unlocking realms beyond our sight—
Not sleep, nor dream, but pure return—
To the field before all forms were born.
The self dissolves, like morning mist
Inside that waiting void.

What lies beyond the final beat?
Not heaven crowned, nor judgment throne,
But vastness without edge or bounds
Where meaning ends, yet love remains,
And yearning rests in the Source again.

A pause between what is and was,
The spirit loosens, slow and free.
All time collapses into now,
And being sheds its need for name.

Then what was "I" begins to fade,
Released from form, from time, from frame.
And in that step beyond all steps—
We fade, and yet—remain.

***

In death, we rise not up but in—
The soul persists, not yet undone
An echo in the Dreamer's field,
The One who dreams all dreaming souls.

Seeker turn to page 60
Chapter 13 : Mind

CHAPTER 36
Birth

"The silence breaks with tender scream,
A breath begins where none had stirred.
An ancient spark now dressed in skin—
Clings to the breast in primal yearning."
– Primordial Lullaby

When light awakened the shrouded eyes,
And air became the soul's first wine,
We had no fear, but knew the beat—
That sings before the mind can think.

Chapter 36: Birth

One must be woven into weight,
To walk the path of pain into form.
From breathless stars to tender moans,
The soul accepts its cage of flesh.
The body answers heaven's call,
By weeping into trembling hands—
Alive, afraid, and fully here.
Yet in the space between two hearts,
A cosmos whispers, "you are here."

Within the womb of wordless peace,
We drifted, curled in sacred dark.
The soul untouched by light or limb,
Still glowing from its astral path.
No hunger yet, no aching bone—
A calm before the storm.

Pain opens wide the gate to life,
A path of blood, of breath, of flame.
The scream, like thunder, splits the silence,
And in its echo, life is named—
The soul now forged into "I am."

A breath, a cry, a crack in time—
The silence ruptures into form.
What rises here will bend the world—
Soft, small—yet wholly formed.

We are not born to simply be,
But to remember what was lost.
Each child holds what time once hid—
A whisper older than its name.

***

Let birth be flame, not blank design—
A soul returning, clothed in ache.
Each breath a stroke across the void—
A tender gaze that blinks "hello."

Seeker turn to page 142
Chapter 35 : Death

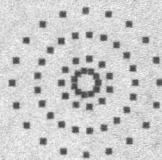

CHAPTER 37
THE THOUGHT

"Some stars were born from thought alone,
Not light, not dust, but pure intent.
Such is the mind, when left to blaze,
It births, it kills, it binds us all."
- The source within: I am the One.

No latch, no knock—one spark.
It ghosts across the mind.
In one swift, wordless curve,
The soul concedes its mold.

Chapter 37: The Thought

One must confront the wandering spark,
Before it wears the face of fact.
It slips inside—unbidden, swift;
Thought sets the stage before we act;
We trade its courtesy for reign.
We dine on schemes it plated first,
Raise glasses to our masterstroke,
Each toast already in the script—
Every word, each letter—staged.

In stillness, something stirs,
Before the cry, before the cut.
Ideas glide like silent owls,
Through corridors of thought.
To think is not to know—
But to witness genesis in hush.

Thought hums one pitch behind the bone;
We slide the fader for a softer whisper,
Or yank the sliders, beg for roar—
It flattens back to even calm,
An endless—flatline tone.

Thoughts combine to spark ideas;
Some carry hidden mold,
Others swell with lucid sap.
Worship them—court disaster.

When thinking fades,
A secret surfaces in calm.
In pause, the Witness stands—
In silence, the observer wakes.

***

Some thoughts we save, while others raze;
Both levy hidden dues.
Descriptors—restless, steering fate—
Direct each scene we think we choose.

Seeker turn to page 146
Chapter 36 : Birth

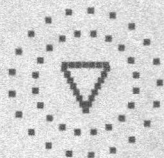

Primal Verses

CHAPTER 38
THE WITNESS

"Behind each thought, a silent eye—
The sovereign seer who never speaks;
It crowns the birth of every word,
Unseen, enthroned in stillness."
- From "Who Is My Witness?"

When mind grows still
And chatter fades to hush,
Something remains—watching,
The One—eternal.

Chapter 38: The Witness

One must find the silent seer,
The Witness to thought at rest.
Not maker, not the made,
But the field where I awaken.
In the gaps of tumbling speech,
The Witness waits, unmoved.
Neither born nor dying,
The observer of all dreams—
The Self that simply is.

Who sees the seer seeing?
Who watches thoughts arise
Like clouds across a boundless sky?
Not mind—for mind is seen.
Not thought—for thought is known.
The Witness bears no name.

In meditation's quiet hour,
When breath becomes a gentle wave,
The Witness wakes—an eye that peers into void,
Not separate from what it sees,
Yet stainless in the flow of change.

Every feeling, each drifting memory,
Each pulse within the flesh—
All are witnessed by the One—
Unbound, beholding the whole.

The Witness judges not, chooses not;
Watching joy and sorrow alike.
Attention calls the Witness forth—
Without focus, the Witness dims.

***

In the space between waking and dream,
You, the reader of these words—
The Witness recognizing Self
In the very act of knowing.

Seeker turn to page 150
Chapter 37 : The Thought

CHAPTER 39
THE WILL

"The muscle tenses with intent—
Will moves the hand that signs the page.
Behind each act, a force decides:
Push through, or let the moment pass."
- The Voice Behind the Act

When flesh meets wall,
And spirit says, "keep going."
A hidden self must choose again:
To yield, or to endure.

Chapter 39: The Will

One must grip the wheel—
Before the crash, before the cliff.
Will cuts through doubt,
Pulls the trigger,
Signs the deed,
Says yes when every nerve cries, "stop."
The Witness sees, but Will decides.
Without Witness—there is no path.
Without Will—there is no step.

Some dawns, Will rises fierce—
Tearing dream from the drowsy mind.
Other times, it whispers soft:
"Tomorrow, not today."
Yet through the quake of doubt,
The work begins again.

Will dares: "One more step."
Even cowards hear it ring.
Courage rides upon its echo—
Not formed in thought,
But summoned from the depths.

Will carves a destiny,
Or yields to comfort's call.
Every choice cracks the old mold,
Each act becomes the chisel.

The strong Will bends but does not break,
The weak Will snaps at first strain.
But neither state is final—
For Will is Self in action.

***

Will deepens where words dissolve—
Not in force, but focus.
The Witness watches; Will commands,
While Ego fights to seize the "I."

Seeker turn to page 154
Chapter 38 : The Witness

CHAPTER 40

THE EGO

"The mask believes it is the face—
Ego whispers: 'I am king,'
While the Witness sleeps and the mind grows wild,
The false Self claims the throne,"
- From the Chronicles of Deception

When thought proclaims itself the law,
And calls itself by name,
The impostor stirs—
Ego claws to reign.

Chapter 40: The Ego

One must see the thief within,
Who blinds the Witness at the gate.
Ego dons the crown of "I,"
Each thought is claimed as its own,
Binds Will in chains and mocks the seer.
It builds castles from ideas,
Defends illusions never born,
And wages war on self—delusion—
The tyrant born from within.

Ego thrives on borrowed standing,
Measuring worth by what it lacks.
It gathers praise like hoarded treasure,
Shields itself from honest blame.
Each scar inscribed as sacred proof,
Each victory—divine decree.

Watch the tyrant primp and posture,
Hungry for its next acclaim.
It dazzles the eye of the Witness,
Leashes Will to chase desires—
But when silence falls—what "I" remains?

The Ego promises control,
But weaves a net of chains.
It paints the world in black and white,
While living truth moves through the gray.

It screams, "I must survive!"
As silence grows,
It grips stray threads of memory
And struts into the dream.

***

When Ego's fever finally breaks,
The Witness clears; the Will stands strong.
Beneath the tyrant's hollow crown—
Lies what was always there: the One.

Seeker turn to page 158
Chapter 39 : The Will

Primal Verses

CHAPTER 41:
THE DREAM

"Between the tick of mortal clocks,
A silent arch appears;
A dream—a breach into the path,
From timeless self—the soul."
- Verses of the Veiled Moon

The seeker slips inside,
Hands free of daylight's weight.
The luminous unknown invites
A deeper pulse to rise.

Chapter 41: The Dream

One must yield to the tidal dark,
Slip beneath the waking crust,
Find the rift between horizons—
Unleash the soul's own storm.
Descend until all colors fade,
Then watch new spectra bloom like dawn;
Where form dissolves in liquid light,
Until the body's borders blur,
And breath expands into constellation.

In galleries of star-born mind,
We trace the tapestry of awe;
Threads of vision twist as keys,
Unlatching gates beyond the veil,
Where thunder rings behind the brow,
Resonating through the soul.

Who speaks within the velvet void
When logic bows to truth's swift call?
Secrets drift like ancient smoke,
Bearing scripts from depths unknown—
Where seekers find their Source.

Beyond the reach of waking thought,
The other world stands revealed,
Where souls are free,
And time is an illusion.

Amid the lucid and the Astral planes,
No thought remains—just knowing;
Mirage recedes, and
Source glints through the void.

***

Through dreams we feast on essence,
Truth streams for those who listen;
Revealing our soul to Self,
Where mortals meet the Divine.

Seeker turn to page 162
Chapter 40 : The Ego

CHAPTER 42
NIGHT TERROR

"Through terror's gate, the spirit falls,
Into the realm of hungry eyes—
Where demi-gods in shadows roam,
And dread refines the One."
- Echoes from the Astral Deep

The seeker, naked, tumbles down,
Through ethereal winds that howl,
Where entities of darkest hue
Strip the Ego bare.

Chapter 42: Night Terror

One must face the terror threshold,
While flesh lies frozen, paralyzed,
In Astral depths where terror-bringers
Make their presence known.
Where spectral currents pull and tear,
And consciousness begins to bleed,
At last the trembling seeker learns—
Terror guards the sacred gate
To realms beyond all mortal fear.

When dark watchmen grant safe passage,
New territories stretch afar—
Where consciousness explores freely
Each distant realm and star.
The shadow guardians step aside,
Their sacred work complete.

What resonates when the trial concludes
And the purified soul shines bright?
A boundless voice of blessed tenderness
Guides the newborn light,
"Enter now—your true domain."

In realms beyond all form,
Terror births the sacred flame;
Where consciousness remembers
Its forgotten cosmic name.

The trembling mind, once fearful,
Emerges from the fall,
Forever touched by what it learned—
Terror's ancient call.

***

In terror's sacred crucible,
The soul learns to transcend;
What seems like torment to the mind
Sets the spirit free to ascend.

Seeker turn to page 166
Chapter 41 : The Dream

CHAPTER 43
ASTRAL

"Beyond the mortal vision,
Where thought becomes reality,
The astral plane awaits the soul
Whose earthly work has just begun.
- Chronicles of the Ethereal Voyager

The seeker leaves the flesh behind,
Through the silver cord that binds,
Into realms of endless light,
Where time and space unwind.

Chapter 43: Astral

One must traverse the astral plane,
Where every thought takes form,
The wanderer finds the gateway wide
To dimensions yet unknown.
No flesh to bind, no earth to hold—
Consciousness takes flight
To territories where the soul
Becomes pure light.

Through astral currents, swift and bright,
The spirit learns to soar,
Past sleeping souls and ancient guides,
To realms where cosmic secrets hide—
Each realm a tome of hidden lore,
A voyage to Infinity's shore.

What pulses within the astral wind,
Where ancient spirits roam?
The heartbeat of eternity
Guiding pilgrims safely home:
"Merge with what you've always been."

In sanctuary beyond all form,
Where spirit knows its name,
Divinity reveals its sacred grace—
The IS, the One, the Self—embrace.

Down the silver cord returns the soul,
Bearing whispers from the void,
Forever changed by the Source's touch—
The soul awakened and transformed.

***

Through astral storms and psychic rain,
Where time dissolves into dream,
The soul returns to primal origin
Within the Ones' convergent stream.

Seeker turn to page 170
Chapter 42 : Night Terror

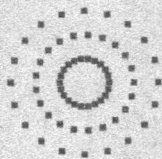

CHAPTER 44
IS

"In the beginning was the Word,
And the Word is existence pure;
Before all form and name arose,
The silent IS breathed forth the worlds."
— Primal Testament

When thought dissolves,
And IS returns to Source,
We touch the face of what we are,
Before the first Word spoke.

Chapter 44: IS

One must descend through layers of illusion—
Through all that seems and all that changes—
To touch the depth that knows no bottom,
Within being's infinite embrace.
Here stands the IS beyond duality,
A presence closer than your skin,
Untouched by birth or dissolution,
Eternal witness, ever watching,
The silent root of what you are.

When silence speaks its deepest truth,
And emptiness reveals its fullness,
We smile at the hide-and-seek of Self,
The game where nothing was concealed;
The IS simply is—nothing more—
And nothing more is needed.

What wonder IS?
When Self yields to the eternal,
Like silence cradling every sound,
Yet brushed by none that rise and fade,
The IS immaculate, complete.

In spaces wide as unborn sky,
Where being knows its boundless nature,
We glimpse the Source of all existence
That needs no thought to validate.

Within the womb of endless quiet,
Where IS reveals its ageless light,
Beyond the reach of doubt or knowing,
We are the deathless, the eternal.

***

When all illusions find their ending,
What remains but boundless IS—
The Source that dreams all seeming worlds,
The deathless watching death itself.

Seeker turn to page 174
Chapter 43 : Astral

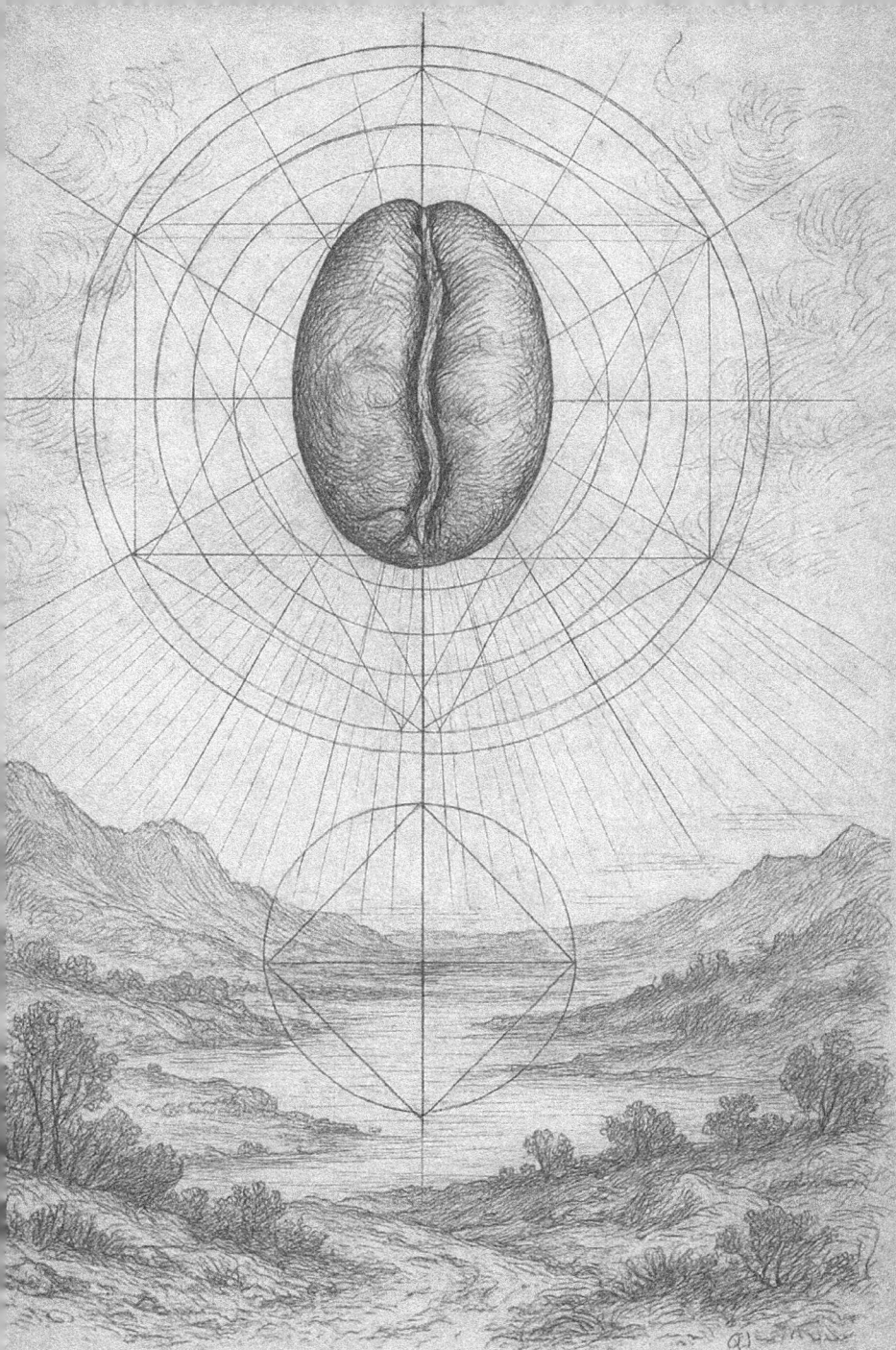

Chapter 45
Coffee

"From bitter beans ground fine as dust,
We brew the elixir of wakeful hours,
Each cup a bridge from dream to deed,
Where thought meets flesh in sacred union."
- Scrolls of the Daily Grind

As morning dreams dissolve to vapor,
And spirit craves its earthly anchor,
We find our altar in the cup,
That tethers souls to the pulse of life.

Chapter 45: Coffee

One must taste the darkness made divine—
Each drop a testament to our struggle,
We swallow our reflection
And taste the price of being awake.
This brew becomes our sacred potion
For work our deeper selves have chosen,
So we can build our mortal empires,
While mist ascends like burning prayers
At the altar of the everyday.

Through ritual of morning's sacrament,
We trade our dreams for bitter wages.
Each sip—a debt we pay to daylight,
That binds us to our chosen burden.
Until we pulse with caffeine—
The engine of our suffering.

What paradox makes gods of servants
Who toil in fields of finite time?
Through humble work and mindful presence
We taste forever in the now—
Transcendence in the trivial.

Yet in this sacred contradiction,
Between the blessing and the curse,
We find the middle path of brew—
Too little lulls the soul;
Too much jars the mind.

In temples of the daily grind,
We share our universal need—
All who crave this black ambrosia
Know the price of staying human.

***

Through beans transformed by fire and time,
We gulp what makes us mortal gods—
Each cup holds earth's eternal promise:
That dust can dream of touching stars.

Sage turn to page 194
Chapter 48 : Hope

Primal Verses

Chapter 46
Duality

"Where darkness learns to taste the light,
And joy unearths its hidden pain,
Each heartbeat writes the cosmic law—
That nothing exists in vain."
- Chronicles of the Eternal Wheel

When opposites reveal their secret,
And the Witness grasps the balance whole,
We dance between the twin extremes,
As all divisions heal in the One.

Chapter 46: Duality

One must embrace the cosmic wheel
Where suffering births the seed of joy.
In vast domains of consciousness,
Each star ignites a choice: night or day.
The Witness sees, the Ego claims,
Will decides while thought creates—
All dancing in the spiral's grip
Of paradox that makes us whole—
Here nothing stands—yet all things kneel.

As shadow leans to kiss the flame,
And contrast ceases to divide,
While silence speaks and noise finds peace,
The truth emerges from the lie,
Until we grasp the hidden law:
What seemed two was always one.

The void whispers what Duality speaks—
Like twin stars bound in sacred orbit,
We spiral through the cosmic dance;
Where every choice becomes a thread
In fate's eternal tapestry.

Between the heights of bliss and dread,
We taste all flavors—love and rage.
On Astral tides we drift and turn
Through the cycles of eternal change.

Deep in the Source that dreams all worlds,
We find ourselves both dust and gods—
Each soul that dares to glimpse between
Finds all divisions melt away.

***

Beyond the dance of yes and no,
We touch the Source of all that is—
Each soul becomes a bridge between
The One that dreams itself as two.

Seeker turn to page 178
Chapter 44 : IS

Chapter 47
Solitude

"Within the soul's most sacred space,
Where healing thoughts drift soft and slow,
Each ripple marks the gentle void—
Yet comfort weaves its golden cage."
– Hermit's Testament

When human comfort turns to ash,
And spirit walks the desert's spine,
We taste the thirst for hidden truth,
As solitude is our shrine.

Chapter 47: Solitude

One must embrace the void with open arms,
Yet guard against its hungry depths.
In silence, truth begins to whisper,
But whispers can become our chains.
The seeker finds their truest voice
When only echo walks beside them.
Such is the paradox of solitude:
We claim the All, yet forfeit many—
And wonder if the One can love.

We venture past the hive of thought,
Where naked truth strips seekers bare,
But pride, coiled in gilt bars of quiet,
Poisons wells once crystal pure—
The self, seeking a perfect mirror
Finds its reflection warped to terror.

When Ego melts into voiceless wax,
The spirit hunts a buried spark.
Between the noise of self-deception
And stillness of the Witness,
We touch the source of I.

Yet in sacred silence, the Witness sees
Through the illusion of the seeker.
The path that seems so personal
Belongs to the One—Divine Dreamer.

The One who sits in stillness deep
Perceives what rushing souls ignore—
But wisdom earned in that still place
Burns with unrelenting bliss.

***

And so we learn—in sacred isolation
We touch the primal wound:
The source of all creation
Aches to be consumed—by love.

Seeker turn to page 186
Chapter 46 : Duality

Chapter 48
Hope

"What logic declares impossible,
The heart insists must be.
Where reason ends its dominion,
Hope begins its tyranny."
- Fragments of the Unconquered

When foundations fall
And purpose fades,
We balance on the edge of night
Where hope summons the divine.

Chapter 48: Hope

One must hope when hope seems madness,
Where doubt invades each tender heart.
In graveyards stripped of bloom,
The soul still burns bright.
This hope defies the end of time,
As stars rage against the dark—
Against the void's eternal call,
We sing our stubborn song
Until hope conquers all.

Across the wasteland of the mind,
We guard the flame once called delusion.
Each breath defies their certainty,
Each heartbeat proves them false.
For spirits learn to feast on faith
And transcend what fools decree impossible.

What force sustains the hoping soul
When all the world calls hope naive?
Like light that pierces prison walls,
We grow where cowards dare not stand—
Each loss becomes our treasure map.

Between the real and never-was,
Hope becomes our sacred curse—
To taste what others dare not dream,
Against reality's iron will.

In gardens of the faithful heart,
We find our strength within—
For every soul that dares to hope
Makes reality their dream.

***

Where martyrs burn for causes lost,
We light the fires of the damned—
Until life's twisted logic proves—
The answer lives in those who choose to hope.

Sage turn to page 198
Chapter 49 : Despair

CHAPTER 49
DESPAIR

"Night pours down like iron rain,
Each drop a silent, sinking stone,
Hope dissolves to bitter stain,
Leaves spirit drowning, cold, alone."
- Laments of the Forsaken

When light deserts weary sight,
And hearts implode in crushing pain,
We drift where broken daylight dies,
Through realms where only shadows reign.

Chapter 49: Despair

One must face the abyss that yawns,
Where nothing answers desperate calls.
In caverns carved by pure anguish,
The soul confronts its null reply.
Here truths burden our fragile frame,
Like weights upon a drowning chest.
Across gray wastes devoid of name,
We stumble blind through numbing pain,
Beneath the crushing weight of loss.

When dreams we built with tender care
Dissolve like mist in morning air,
And all our hopes return to ash—
What's left when even faith is lost?
While every vision that we held
Lies broken, shattered, and exposed.

Where time reduces all to dust,
And ticking seconds grind the will,
We feel the planet's patient rust
Consuming plans that we have built,
Till all that stands is mortal sin.

Yet in choices sown with fevered hands,
The harvest comes, severe and bare;
Debts long ignored now must be paid,
And wisdom comes too late to trade.

When all facades have fallen away,
The void converses, cold and clear:
We hear what darkness has to say
To hearts that face the void alone.

***

In darkness deeper than the grave,
Where the raven hungers for the cry,
We forge our strength from deepest pain—
For phoenixes must first die.

Sage turn to page 202
Chapter 50 : Illusion

CHAPTE 50
ILLUSION

"Minutes flow like endless streams,
Hours slip through mortal hands,
Time weaves fate with golden strands,
Life unfolds in fleeting dreams."
- Scrolls of the Deceived

Shadows dance where light should be,
Each beam reveals what darkness hides,
Between what's real and illusion,
We glimpse what we refuse to see.

Chapter 50: Illusion

One must awaken from the dream,
To find the One, embrace the many.
Each seeker moves through veils of light
Where silence swallows every sound.
The dreamer wakes to find they are
The dream itself, the stage, the play—
Neither distance near nor truth afar,
When all is One and One is All,
And form itself begins to fray.

In labyrinths of shifting thought,
We seek the truth but grasp at foam.
Like dew, truth disappears,
It vanishes at dawn.
We build the maze where we get lost,
And pay illusion's hidden cost.

The self is a river, never stone,
As cells renew in flowing streams.
While ego trims its borrowed crown,
No core remains, though we believe
We are the stillness in the flow.

Between the dreamer and the dream,
Where vision cloaks itself as real,
Emotions fall like autumn leaves—
Ripples on a phantom stream.

Knowledge builds its ivory towers,
Each fact a brick that blocks the view.
The mind that clings to lessons learned
Finds wisdom slipping through.

***

Each color thinks it paints the world,
While every hue insists it's true,
Till spectrum fades to purest white—
The One that births both dark and light.

Sage turn to page 210
Chapter 52 : Aging

CHAPTER 51
REALITY

"The mind that watches, shapes the seen,
Observer's role in the machine,
Consciousness threads the fabric tight,
Between the dark and quantum light."
- Chronos Revelations

In bits of quantum information,
Reality finds its foundation,
Each qubit sings the cosmic verse,
A binary of the universe.

Chapter 51: Reality

One must transcend the finite cage,
Beyond these scaffolds built of dust,
Where spirit finds its sacred trust.
The heart discovers its true place.
Oh, how these realms extend,
Like bridges toward the Divine.
Past what our mortal eyes can see,
Until we truly learn to find,
The patterns—always there—designed.

Through currents of the Hidden Mover,
Where motion leads the cosmic dance,
Within the subtle pull of gravity,
In rhythms hidden from our sight;
Until we fuse with what we see—
We are the motion, raw and free.

What substance forms our very being,
When vibration sets the key?
In frequencies beyond mortal hearing,
We tune to what we're meant to be
Across all dimensions of reality.

When consciousness begins to swell,
And opens doors we cannot see,
Ethereal realms where spirits tell
Of worlds beyond our earthly shell.

Where motion threads the fabric true,
And vibration voices the sacred sound,
Through ether's halls of endless view,
Our consciousness returns—unbound.

***

What seems so solid, blunt, and real
Is consciousness in masquerade;
We are vibration and the motion—
One timeless tremor we call soul.

Seeker turn to page 190
Chapter 47 : Solitude

Chapter 52

Aging

"Through time we flow,
Watch years grow.
Through space we glide,
With Age as our guide."
- Songs of Time

Remember when we felt so young?
When every hope was freshly sung.
Those days of time that felt so vast—
Too bad such moments couldn't last.

Chapter 52: Aging

One must ask what it means to age and grow—
To age means watching beauty fade,
To grow means seeing what we've made.
Though life chases death with reckless speed,
Something deeper starts to grow.
Feel the weight along the crooked spine?
See the face that once was mine?
Hear the whispers of decay?
Time will have its way.

Our bodies are a temple,
Yet we rarely step inside.
Listen to the sacred chambers—
The heart that beats with pride.

Do you see another wrinkle?
You bear the scars of sacred time!
Will you cover up your journey,
Or stand with sacred courage, brave?

Remember when the days felt long?
When every dream was fresh and strong?
Now moments blur, and seasons fly—
We wave our younger selves goodbye.
Yet time moves fast while memories stay,
Still echoing from yesterday.

Time carved us into something fierce—
Each wrinkle earned through blood and tears.
Yet wisdom comes with every scar,
And beauty lies in who we are.

***

Do you dream of stopping time?
Of keeping youth forever prime?
But age shows why we came to earth,
Through death—rebirth.

Sage turn to page 218
Chapter 54 : Destiny

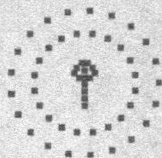

CHAPTER 53

HUMANITY

"We are the sinner and the saint,
The gentle brush with violent paint,
Of broken dreams and soaring flight,
In humanity we burn so bright."
- Chronicles of the Human Soul

When minutes stretch to endless years,
And decades pass like fleeting tears,
We chase the clock that won't stand still,
Through ages carved by human will.

Chapter 53: Humanity

One must find in mankind's core
The peace we seek, the endless war,
Where mercy floods through our veins,
While cruelty carves a bitter stain.
We reach for heaven, fall to hell,
Have sacred stories we must tell.
We give our love, then hearts may break;
The gentle touch may turn to quake,
Such is the price of being great.

The meek will bow while the bold stand tall,
One heart can house both rise and fall.
We build with hope, then raze with rage,
Script love and hate on the same page.
In every soul a dual flame,
Both blessed and cursed, yet both the same.

Strange beasts are we—so wise, so blind,
Who speak of light, yet maim in kind,
We scale the peaks of noble thought,
Then sell our souls for trinkets bought;
Blind to the cost of what we sought.

From ash to gold, from hate to love,
We dive below, we soar above;
We move through time's unending flow,
Where angels dance with devils' glow.

So in this dance of high and low,
We reap the seeds that we must sow;
This tension shapes us whole,
Contradictions forge the soul.

***

In mirrors of humanity,
We glimpse both beast and deity.
The fool, the sage, the weak, the strong,
All share one pulse, one human song.

Seeker turn to page 206
Chapter 51 : Reality

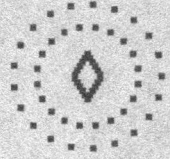

Chapter 54
Destiny

"Stars align in cosmic dance,
Drawing souls through mortal chance;
Each heart keeps time with ageless song—
Where fate and freedom both belong."
- Prophecies of the Cosmic Wheel

Purpose calls through shadowed years,
Threaded light begins to shine;
Between what chance and fate endear,
We walk the trembling cosmic line.

Chapter 54: Destiny

One must trust the inner call,
That whispers through our mortal years;
For seeds of destiny still grow,
Long before we learned to feel.
Each moment holds both chance and plan,
As starlight guides our earthly way.
What's written in the cosmic span
Unfolds through choices made today—
We choose to be, or not to be.

In landscapes drawn by cosmic hand,
Each crossroads bows to what was planned.
We bloom exactly as we're meant,
Our purpose written, Heaven-sent.
Until we dare to trust the way,
That guides us through each sacred day.

What powers guide our mortal days?
How does chance reveal our destined ways?
Like rivers seeking ocean's shore,
We follow paths we barely see,
Yet fulfill our prophecy.

Between free will and fated thread,
Where destiny reveals its hand,
Life opens up its secret code
Where luck and time collide.

Woven tight in starlit schemes,
Each thread fulfills celestial dreams.
Our purpose set in ages past,
The cosmic stage has set our cast.

***

We dance the steps the stars have planned,
Sometimes we soar, sometimes we fall.
Not every soul bears glory's brand—
Some fall so others might prevail.

Sage turn to page 222
Chapter 55 : Choice

Primal Verses

Chapter 55
Choice

"Every choice branches wide,
Creating worlds we've never tried,
Present moments hold the primal key
To unlock what we will be."
- Book of Infinite Possibility

So many roads spread out ahead,
Which way should weary footsteps take?
Between the heart and restless head,
Where hopes and trembling fears awake.

Chapter 55: Choice

One must honor what feels right,
When branching paths appear in sight,
We choose the dreams we dare to chase,
And forge our legend in the stars.
In choice we claim our power true,
To craft the path we're walking through.
The future bends to meet our way,
Our reign of choice begins today.

Through paths that twist and intertwine,
We claim the road called mine;
Each door swings open, others shut,
As destiny follows our chosen route.
Our lives become what we decide,
When truth and choice walk side by side.

What power lies in one small choice,
When time itself must hear our voice?
Like artists painting destiny,
We craft tomorrow's mystery
From present moment's energy.

Between the now and what may be,
Where time demands we take our stand;
Each moment holds the power free
To shape our destiny's decree.

This single moment holds all power
To reshape our destined hour,
In choice's crucible we find
The alchemy of heart and mind.

***

We'll never know what might have been,
Nor paths we chose not to begin;
Choice is the mystery within—
A sacred ache that whispers — Hand of God.

Sage turn to page 226
Chapter 56 : Kiss

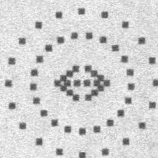

Chapter 56
Kiss

"Gentle kisses, soft and slow,
Tell the tales hearts long to know,
In this moment so sublime,
Souls begin to rhyme."
- Chronicles of Sacred Touch

Where gentle breath begins to meet,
Time itself forgets to beat;
Hearts unite in yearning bliss—
Heaven found within a kiss.

Chapter 56: Kiss

One must treasure the first kiss,
When racing hearts endure,
In trembling breath of bliss,
Love begins anew.
Virgin spirits soar,
Two souls breathe as one,
Holy vows unspoken,
Sacred silence broken—
Love forevermore.

On tender lips we meet
A pledge from heart to mind.
Each kiss makes love complete,
In love's enduring way.
Our spirits learn to speak
What words can never say.

Love connects what seems apart,
Every kiss contains the whole.
Atoms dance like lovers;
As Two converge to forge One soul,
In love's most sacred art.

Through all the years that rise and fall,
The kiss remains love's truest call—
A sacred gift that crowns us all,
Love's silent verse for everyone.

In kiss we see ourselves
Reflected in another's grace.
In love's eternal space,
We truly know each other.

***

What makes us One?
This universal need for grace—
In gentle kiss, love's work is done.

Sage turn to page 230
Chapter 57 : Loss

CHAPTER 57
LOSS

"When all the tears have dried to salt,
When all the screams exhausted sound,
What's left isn't a sorrow or a fault—
Just emptiness, profound."
- Verses from the Void

Tiny fingers never curled,
Little feet that never ran;
Sweet face that never smiled,
Little soul in heaven's span.

Chapter 57: Loss

One must understand the loss
Of moments spent in vain,
How time extracts its sacrifice
From pleasure and from pain.
Each second is a debt
We never can repay,
The bill that we beget
Will come to claim what's due.

Seeds of sorrow take their root,
Growing wild in fertile pain.
What we planted bears no fruit,
Only thorns and foul remorse.
We tend this garden of our grief—
Where healing offers no relief.

Assets crumble overnight,
Every coin reveals the cost.
Pride falls hard, accounts stand empty—
Years of careful planning lost,
What we saved, we can't get back.

Deeper debts outlast the purse—
The words we left unsaid,
The chances killed by dread,
What once was—
Echoes in each falling tear.

Water runs but never back,
Youth flows to the endless sea;
What we had we can't retract,
Gone eternally.

***

From every end, a new beginning;
From every death, rebirth—
Loss reveals life's deeper meaning:
The sacred measure of our worth.

Sage turn to page 234
Chapter 58 : War

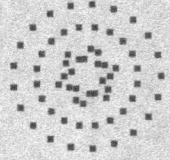

CHAPTER 58
WAR

"Thunder rolls through blood-soaked earth,
Where brothers' eyes burn cold as ice,
Each soul forgets its gentle birth
And pays war's terrible dark price."
- Chronicles of the Crimson Dawn

When peace abandons earth below,
And war drums sound their deadly call,
We drift between the true and false,
Where angels fear war's deadly waltz.

Chapter 58: War

One must know what war will take,
When tender hearts learn how to kill.
In fields where angels weep and kneel,
As darkness claims each grieving soul.
Like predators we mark our land,
While mothers mourn within their hell
For children buried in the mud.
As masters play their games of state,
War leaves the fields with death alone.

When weapons write the law in blood,
And smoke obscures the sun,
Each prayer becomes a desperate cry—
From lips that taste of blood,
Where young souls march to die
With honor—duty as their shield.

Pretty posters paint war bright
With heroes gleaming, courage strong,
But truth reveals a different sight—
That glory lives in patriot's song
To mask the horror from the mind.

While soldiers bleed on foreign land,
Some count their coins with silent glee,
Building wealth with bloody hands
From others' pain, from tragedy.

The battle-worn see different skies
That witnessed hell across the sea,
Nothing here can harmonize
With what war has made of them.

***

Scars fade, seasons turn;
From ash, new life will bloom.
What wisdom did the fallen learn?
Between Heaven and Hell is War.

Sage turn to page 238
Chapter 59 : Religion

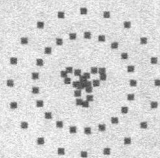

CHAPTER 59
RELIGION

"Though prophets wrote of divine will,
Each soul must find their own way,
The sage's journey shapes divine,
As truth evolves from yesterday."
- The Sage's Testament

Where orthodoxy builds its rigid wall,
And preachers claim to know the mind of God,
We balance faith of old with thoughts today,
As our spirit yearns to name the truth—someday.

Chapter 59: Religion

One must witness how the faithful bind,
Young spirits in the chains of holy words,
The poison spreads where doctrine flows,
And fills young minds with lead.
It spreads before young minds mature—
From those who preach but harbor loathing.
Children drown in holy scripture,
While curiosity meets swift disgrace,
And freedom dies beneath religious brand.

Past altars where the faithful bow,
The spirit searches for its home.
Each doctrine claims its truth is sound,
Yet truth needs no cathedral wall—
No mosque can cage enlightened soul,
When inner wisdom freely grows.

True holiness lives in the deed,
Not in the sacred book we read.
Compassion breaks religious chains,
Puts God within our daily reach,
When kindness grows while dogma fails.

Hatred dressed as righteous thought
Destroys what God in love has wrought.
They teach that flesh is born to sin—
And kill all joy before life can begin.

Fear becomes their holy tool,
To turn free souls into bound fools.
Hellfire preached to small children
Forges chains around them all.

***

Sunday saints with Monday sins
Show where true religion ends.
They preach of love but practice hate—
Heaven's door becomes hell's gate.

Sage turn to page 250
CONTINUE

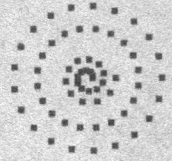

CHAPTER 60
The Source

"Before the dawn of time and space,
Before the silence learned to cry,
There flows the current with no end—
The Source of everything."
- Primordial Mysteries

Between the Zero and the One,
The Source is found.
The mover that itself stays still,
Bends existence to its will.

Chapter 60: The Source

What current runs through all that is?
What Force stirs the endless void?
By neither time nor death destroyed,
It flows through everything,
The motion that precedes all motion,
The stirring in the space between,
Like some eternal, vast devotion—
The Source of One and everything,
The root of all eternity.

None escape its endless pull,
Making empty spaces full.
Beyond the rim of time and space,
At existence's edge it stays,
Where Zero trembles toward the One—
Infinity has begun.

It moves like wind we cannot see,
This Source that grants reality,
No form, no weight, yet sparks appear,
Foundation-giver, bridge divine,
From void to spark, the perfect line.

Thus the circle closes here,
Where beginning meets its end.
Source and substance, one in motion,
Time and timeless freely blend.

From this current comes all life,
To this current all returns.
In the space between the breathing,
Endless Source forever burns.

***

From void to form, the Source commands,
The bridge where Zero learns to be—
In its eternal motion stands
The seed of all becoming!

Seeker turn to page 214
Chapter 53 : Humanity

CHAPTER 61
THE ONE

"As cosmos spins above,
So cells dance here below.
The Source expresses love—
The One becoming Two."
— The Hermetic Axiom

From Zero's womb springs One divine,
Where star and soul in union shine,
What moves the cosmos moves within—
One Source where all true paths begin.

Chapter 61: The One

One must grasp how Zero multiplies—
In astral depths where silence reigns,
The Source awakens what never dies,
Through Many, One gains its voice.
Within the Source, we each belong,
The IS unfolds the sacred plan,
That bridges God and mortal soul,
Where ancient wisdom speaks the truth—
Immortality.

Through countless selves the One perceives,
What every living soul believes,
In flesh, Divinity resides,
Where primal truth in silence hides,
All paths converge to one true way—
The incarnation of the IS.

From heights divine to matter's core,
The eternal current flows through all,
The Source from which all patterns form,
Where seekers find their hidden core,
The IS within us all.

The void conceives infinity,
All paths return to the Source.
What seems like Many is but One—
The Dreamer dreams alone.

In sacred dance of yes and no,
The seeker threads between extremes,
Until at last the truth breaks through:
"I am the source of all my dreams."

***

As atoms dance like distant stars,
And cells reflect the cosmic whole,
The One dreams through these mortal scars—
The dreamer waking from the fall.

Seeker turn to page 242
Chapter 60 : Source

Primal Verses

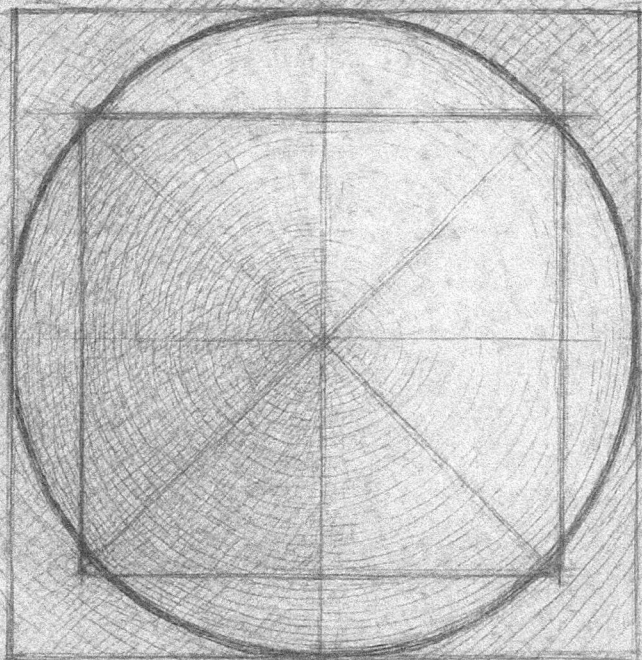

Continue

CONTINUE

Continue the journey through alternative soul paths:

THE SEEKER
Quest for Truth & Unity

Turn to **Page 246** for
Chapter 61: One
Follow Seeker Path

THE WANDERER
Experience & Discovery

Turn to **Page 10** for
Chapter 2: Purpose
Follow Wanderer Path

THE SAGE
Wisdom & Enlightenment

Turn to **Page 14** for
Chapter 3: What is life?
Follow Sage Path

Follow your chosen soul symbol.

JOIN THE PRIMAL VERSES COMMUNITY

Your journey through the 62 chapters of Primal Verses is just the beginning. Join a vibrant community of spiritual seekers, poets, and readers who are expanding the universe of Primal Verses together., visit:

www.primalverses.com

Transform from reader to creator in the Primal Verses community. Our platform provides tools and inspiration for you to craft your own spiritual poetry, guided by the same principles that shaped the original chapters.

Social media reimagined: where every stanza is a post, every verse an interaction, and every human experience finds its voice through poetry.

Welcome to authentic connection through the written word and share it with the world.

PRIMAL VERSES

SERIES 1-6

The complete Primal Verses series will unfold across six transformative volumes, each exploring deeper dimensions of consciousness and human experience.

PUBLICATION TIMELINE

Volume 1: Zero to One - 2005-2025 - 62 chapters
Volume 2: Estimated - 2027 - 61 chapters
Volume 3: Estimated - 2030 - 61 chapters
Volume 4: Estimated - 2033 - 61 chapters
Volume 5: Estimated - 2036 - 61 chapters
Volume 6: Estimated - 2040 - 61 chapters

Community Chapter Creation: **primalverses.com/books**

Help shape the future volumes by submitting chapter titles for unpublished books. Your creative vision could become part of the eternal Primal Verses journey.

Author Reflection

When the first chapters emerged twenty years ago, I knew that structure and foundation would help me create something far more meaningful than regular poetry; by leveraging numerology and systematic architecture.

As a web engineer developing systems by day and mapping consciousness by night, I discovered that the soul responds to the same mathematical precision that creates elegant code. Consciousness itself has architecture—pathways, patterns, and systematic routes that honor how different souls naturally approach truth.

Each chapter follows sacred geometric principles: opening invocation, contextual bridge, core teaching, sacred pause (***), and synthesis—creating temples for consciousness transformation

This creates—spiritual literature that satisfies both skeptical minds and yearning hearts. The mathematical structure is functional, not decorative.

I wanted Primal Verses to reflect that divine order—where every number, sequence, and pattern serves consciousness transformation.

From void to form, from Zero to ONE, the journey continues...

—Andrey Aleshintsev

❋ ✖ | ✝ ◇ | ❦ ✛ ❂ ✤ ❖ ▽ ✖ ▢

-1+3.2-5+4.2+4.7.1.6-6+5.3-7.4

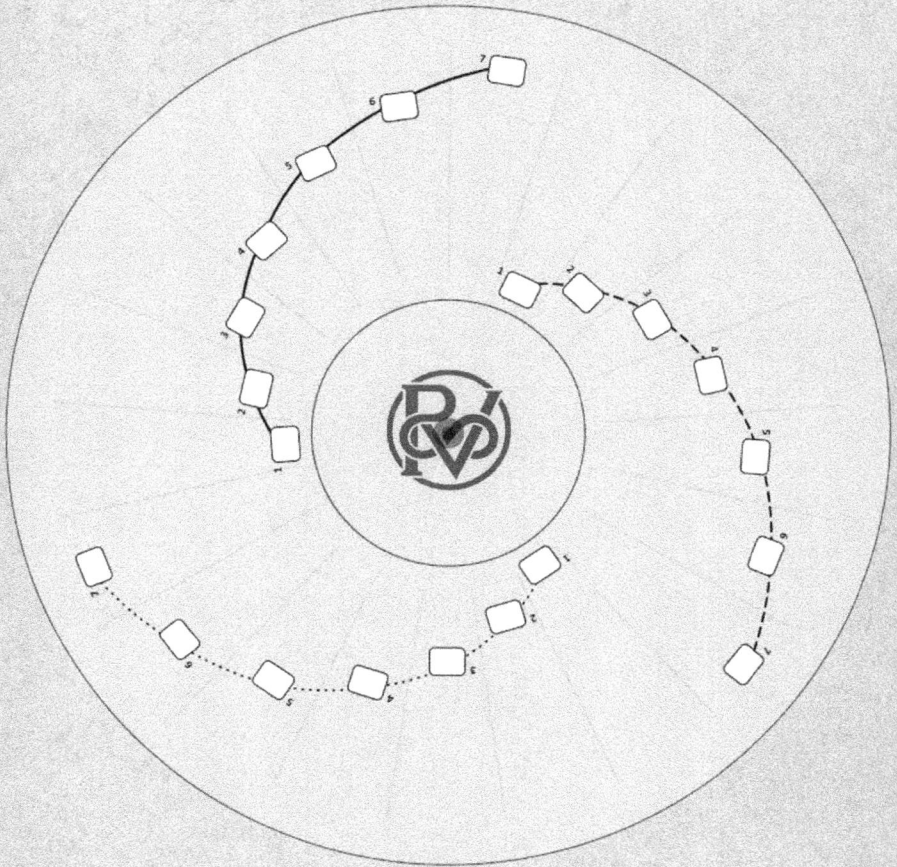